Cheers,
Bitches

ooze Fairy

AIL RECIPE BOOK

FUN
WITH
RUM

Written by Keith Kaczorek
ustrations, Design and Cocktail Tasting
by Michael Q. Ceballos

TABLE OF CONTENTS

Yo Ho Ho It's The Intro.................................... iv
Of Pirates, Patriots & Poets........................... vi
About These Recipes...................................... viii
Top Ten Classics.. 1
Twisted Favorites... 15
Tutti Frutti.. 29
Daiquiri Daiquiri Dock.................................... 43
Tiki Time.. 57
Holiday Cheer... 71
Nice N' Spicy.. 85
Rum Runners... 100
Island Delights.. 114
Get Your Pirate On.. 128
Appendix: Know Your Rums............................. 141
Closing Thoughts... 145

Yo Ho Ho It's The Intro

Right about now you might be asking yourself who is this Booze Fairy and why does he have his own rum cocktail recipe book anyway? Good questions, but essentially irrelevant because if you're reading this a) you've already bought the book and b) we already have your money. Sure you could return it, but is it really worth your time and effort not to mention the additional shipping cost? We're sure you have lots of better things to do like rinsing out your socks, removing unsightly ear hairs or solving the Daily Jumble.

However, in answer to the first question here's...

The Legend Of The Booze Fairy

Known far and wide as the plastered pixie who at one time or another leads most of us astray, the Booze Fairy has a long, colorful history and a singular mission: getting everyone to par-tay!

While some speculate that the Booze Fairy eased the dinosaurs through the trauma of extinction, there is actually no evidence of bars, beer commercials or corner liquor stores in the fossil record. However, by the time primitive man began settling into villages ample evidence exists of the Booze Fairy's influence helping to shape the ancient world. Not only are there numerous examples of pottery that show mankind was getting potted, innumerable tales of Saturday night brawls, questionable dating decisions and rampant keg stands abound in the oral traditions of ancient cultures across the globe. And don't forget the various gods and goddesses who are simply the Booze Fairy in one of his many guises. For example there's the Greek god Bacchus whose revelers held drunken orgies where they devoured live goats, giving rise to the so-called Greek college fraternity culture that survives to this day.

Throughout history one can clearly see the imprint of the Booze Fairy's shaky hand. It's a well-documented fact that Genghis Khan's great marches of conquest started out as pub crawls and that the Booze Fairy himself taught the mongol horde to play beer pong using human heads. The Vikings famously journeyed thousands of miles in open longboats to explore the New World relying solely on the Booze Fairy for navigation. And contrary to popular hippie opinion, the Buddha simply passed out under the Bodhi Tree deep in "meditation" with his tipsy little pal.

In fact it's been scientifically proven that the Booze Fairy is behind literally every human achievement no matter how questionable. After all, what else would lead people to do things like clog dancing, NASCAR or yodeling? When you think about it, how many of us wouldn't even be here if our parents hadn't had a three-way with you-know-who?

Thanks Booze Fairy!

OF PIRATES, PATRIOTS & POETS

When you think about rum, you think about pirates because "yo ho ho and a bottle of tequila" just doesn't sound right. Even though pirates have existed throughout history, they are forever linked in most people's minds to the colonial Caribbean for the obvious reason we can't mention because a certain cartoon mouse guards his intellectual properties like a starved pit bull guards a pork chop.

The whole pirate thing aside, what the heck is rum anyway? Put simply it's an alcoholic beverage made by fermenting and distilling sugarcane juice or molasses. The clear elixir is then often aged in oak barrels. Rum is not only an integral part of Caribbean culture, but of many Latin American cultures and of Canada's Maritime Provinces as well. Most rum is produced in the Western Hemisphere, but some variation is also produced in sugar growing countries all over the world, such as the Philippines and India. (see the Appendix at the end of the book for a detailed description of styles and types of rum).

You can think of rum as value-added sugar. The added value being it gets you hammered. Historically it served as a medium of economic exchange which was used, unfortunately, to help fund the African slave trade and American organized crime during Prohibition among other things. On the plus side it also helped support military insurgencies such as the American Revolution and Australia's Rum Rebellion, while no doubt inspiring the insurgents as well. We'll never know how many great patriots were plastered when they charged the British guns. However, it's a sure bet that rum made America great even before there was an America. Drink free or die!

Speaking of those wacky Brits, rum is also famous for its long association with the Royal Navy whose sailors to this day mix rum with water or beer to make their daily grog. Even the crews of Her Majesty's ballistic missile submarines - you know, the ones with the nukes - enjoy a daily ration. Guess it steadies their hands in case they have to push the launch button.

And let's not forget the reams of good writing inspired by this glorious spirit. It's safe to say that rum is truly the drink of poets, because poets will pretty much drink anything. So next time you're enjoying your favorite rum libation, raise a glass to the pirates, patriots and poets who've chugged their rum before you.

Yo ho ho!

ABOUT THESE RECIPES

The Booze Fairy wants to make a few overall points about preparing the recipes in this book. First, he made every effort to keep them as simple and easy as possible. Ditto for the barware and glassware required. This ain't mixology school, boys and girls. It's about having fun with rum, and getting to that fun as expeditiously as possible. That said, a few ingredients in these recipes may require some searching out. But hey no pain no gain, right?

Second, the Booze Fairy wants these recipes to get you where you're going in a timely and efficient manner 'cuz that's how he rolls. Therefore many are a bit stronger than their traditional formulations. If that's not to your liking, feel free to seek out a less potent recipe, ya' lousy commie.

Third, you can pretty much assume you'll need ice for preparing, or serving most of these libations. And if you have the time it also helps to chill your glasses, especially for the frozen drinks.

And when a recipe calls for fruit juice, fresh is always preferred. However, the Booze Fairy realizes this often isn't practical. Fresh apricot nectar or coconut milk? Good luck with that. So just buy it bottled or canned, and enjoy the damn cocktails. And you can freely substitute seltzer or sparkling water wherever club soda is called for.

Finally, only fresh mint will do. Any kind of dried or squeeze tube mint is just plain wrong.

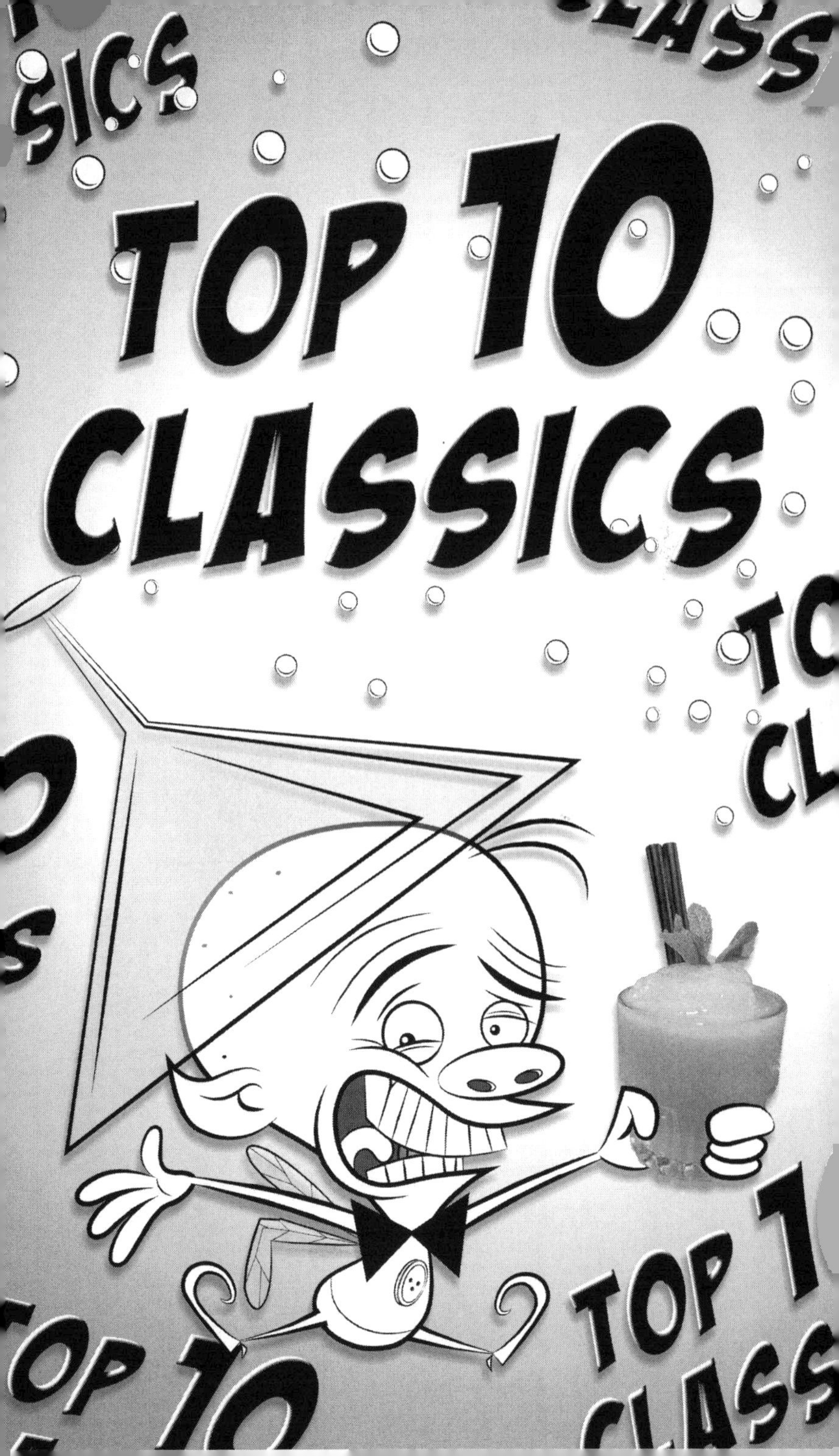
TOP 10
CLASSICS

TOP TEN CLASSICS

Classics are classics for a reason. If you're new to rum cocktails, you could find worse ways to begin your journey than these tried and true favorites. Obviously, some of these would be a natural fit in other categories later in this book and may even be the root of the tree so to speak. However, the Booze Fairy feels it's best to start with the classics and build from there. And who are we mere mortals to argue?

1) RUM & COLA

3 oz. of your favorite rum
your favorite cola
lime slice & maraschino cherry garnish

Pour rum into a tall (tom collins) glass filled with ice, top it with cola and garnish. This simple, yet effective cocktail is a favorite at frat' parties, raves and anywhere else amateurs congregate. Hey, ya' gotta start somewhere.

2) LONG ISLAND ICE TEA

1 oz. light rum
1 oz. vodka
1 oz. gin
1 oz. tequila
1/2 oz. triple sec
1/2 oz. lemon juice
cola
lemon wedges

Mix rum, vodka, gin, tequila, triple sec and lemon juice in a shaker with ice. Pour 1/2 the mixture into tall (tom collins) glass with ice and top off with the cola. Garnish with lemon wedge. NOTE: this recipe makes two cocktails, 'cuz no one the Booze Fairy associates with ever stops at one.

3) MOJITO

2 oz. light rum
2 tbsp. sugar, or simple syrup
10 mint leaves
4 lime wedges
club soda

Muddle (mash) mint leaves and 1 lime wedge in a tall, sturdy glass to release their flavor. Add 2 more lime wedges and sugar or syrup. Muddle again. Fill the glass with ice, pour in the rum and top with club soda. Add more sugar if desired. Garnish with remaining lime wedge. BTW - special Caribbean mojito mint is preferred, but regular old spearmint or peppermint will do the job.

4) DAIQUIRI

2 oz. light rum
1 oz. lime juice
1 oz. simple syrup
lime twist garnish

Mix all ingredients in a shaker with ice, strain into a chilled martini or champagne glass and garnish with lime twist. Then put on your white linen suit and Panama hat and pretend you're in some Havana bar waiting for Papa Hemingway to drop by after a day of marlin fishing.

5) BRASS MONKEY

2 oz. dark rum
2 oz. vodka
2 oz. orange juice
orange slice & maraschino cherry garnish

Mix all ingredients in a shaker with ice,
strain into a tall (tom collins) glass filled
with ice and garnish. Note: if ever there
was a drink to "monkey around with" by
substituting light rum for vodka this is it.

6) MAI TAI

2 oz. light rum
1 oz. dark rum
1 oz. orange curaçao
1 oz. lime juice
1/2 oz orgeat (or Amaretto) liqueur
lime slice & mint sprig garnish
1/2 oz dark rum to float (optional)

Mix rum, curaçao, juice and liqueur in
a shaker with crushed ice. Pour into
a tall (tom collins) glass, float dark
rum on top and garnish. BTW – this is
a great candidate for overproof rum,
but then really, what isn't?

7) PIÑA COLADA

2 oz. light rum
3 oz. pineapple juice
1 oz. coconut cream, or coconut milk
pineapple slice &
maraschino cherry garnish

Mix rum, juice and coconut cream (or milk) in a shaker with crushed ice. Pour into a tall (tom collins) glass and garnish. The traditional presentation calls for a poco grande stemmed glass, but you could serve it in a plastic cup and not hear a complaint.

8) ZOMBIE

2 oz. light rum
1 oz. dark rum
1 oz. orange curaçao
1/2 oz. lemon juice
1/2 oz. lime juice
2 oz. orange juice
2 oz. passion fruit syrup
1/2 oz. grenadine
2 dashes Angostura bitters
mint sprig & seasonal fruit garnish
1/2 oz. overproof rum to float (optional)

Mix all ingredients in a shaker with ice. Strain into a tall (tom collins) glass filled with ice, float 1/2 oz. of over-proof dark rum on top if desired and garnish. Some wild and crazy guys and gals even forego the garnish and just float the overproof rum then light it. CAUTION! Always - please, please, please - wait till a flaming drink burns itself out before drinking. Your eyebrows will thank you.

10

9) BACARDI

3 oz. light rum
1 oz. lemon, or lime juice
1 oz. grenadine

Mix all ingredients in a shaker with ice then strain into a martini or champagne glass. Simple, elegant and so tasty. That's why it's a classic.

10) HURRICANE

2 oz. light rum
2 oz. dark rum
1 oz. overproof light rum
1 oz. lemon juice
1 oz. orange juice
1 oz. passion fruit syrup (or mashed
passion fruit and simple syrup)
splash of grenadine
orange slice & maraschino cherry
garnish

Mix all ingredients in shaker with ice,
strain into a tall (tom collins) glass
filled with ice and garnish. This New
Orleans favorite - sipped from plastic
cups up and down Bourbon St. - will
lift up your shirt, whether it's Mardi
Gras or not.

TWISTED FAVORITES

Rum is a versatile substitute for other spirits and will bring a new twist to your favorite cocktails. Light rum can be substituted for vodka and gin, while golden and darker rums are a fine change of pace for cocktails featuring brandy or whisk(e)y - however you spell it. Here are some of the Booze Fairy's personal faves'. He encourages you to improvise and come up with your own.

1) RUMTINI

3 oz. light rum
1 oz. dry vermouth
dash orange bitters
olive, lemon twist, cocktail onion, or
pickled mushroom garnish

It's the classic martini made with rum instead of vodka or gin. Mix all ingredients in a shaker with ice. Strain into a martini glass with your garnish of choice. You can substitute a dry white wine for vermouth to compliment the rum's sweet smoothness. And remember, regardless of the booze you use everyone looks classy with a martini glass in their hand.

2) RUMLET

3 oz. light rum
1 oz. Rose's lime juice

It's the classic vodka gimlet made with
rum. Mix rum and lime juice over ice in
a short (old-fashioned) glass, or mix
over ice in a shaker and strain into a
martini glass. It's your choice. Since
rum and lime combine so naturally,
this twist is a natural.

3) OLD-FASH-RUMMED

3 oz. golden or dark rum
1/2 tsp. sugar
1 tsp. water
2 dashes bitters
lime peel twist or
maraschino cherry garnish
1 tsp. overproof rum to float
(optional)

It's the classic old-fashioned made with rum instead of whiskey (or brandy if you're in the great state of Wisconsin). In a short (old-fashioned) glass mix sugar, water and bitters until sugar dissolves. Add 2-3 ice cubes, pour in rum, mix well and add garnish. Hardcore rummies can float some overproof rum on top for extra nutrition.

4) RUM ROY

3 oz. golden or dark rum
1 oz. sweet vermouth
2 dashes Angostura bitters
maraschino cherry garnish

It's the classic Rob Roy/Manhattan made with rum instead of scotch or American whiskey. Mix ingredients over ice in a shaker, strain into a martini glass and garnish. The sweetness of the rum and vermouth are a great mix, and once again the martini glass makes you look classy even when you face plant with your pants around your ankles.

5) SCREW-RUMMER

2 oz. light rum
orange juice
orange slice garnish

It's the classic screwdriver made with rum. Fill a tall (tom collins) glass with ice, add rum and top off with orange juice. Stir well and garnish. Easy peezy and, as an added bonus, the vitamin C in the O.J. makes it healthy!

6) RUMMY MARY

2 oz. light rum
your favorite bloody mary mix
celery stick, olive and jalapeño pep-
per garnish

It's the classic bloody mary made with
rum. Fill a tall (tom collins) glass, Mason jar, or tulip glass if you're having
brunch with ice, add rum and your
favorite bloody mary mix - homemade or pre-made - the Booze Fairy
doesn't judge. Mix well and add garnish of your choice. A beer chaser is
a nice compliment.

7) RUMTONIC

2 oz. light rum
tonic water
lime wedge

It's the refreshing summer classic
G&T, or V&T, made with rum. In a
tall (tom collins) glass filled with ice
add rum and top off with tonic water. Squeeze in the juice from the lime
wedge and then add it as a garnish.
Once again it's healthy, since tonic water contains quinine which can
help fight malaria. However, truth be
told modern tonic has nowhere near
enough quinine to actually
be effective.

8) SOURUM

3 oz. light, golden or dark rum
1 oz. lemon juice
1 tbsp. orange juice
1 tbsp. simple syrup, or sugar
orange slice garnish
1 tsp. overproof rum to float (optional)

It's the classic whiskey sour made with rum. Mix ingredients over ice in a shaker. Strain into a short (old-fashioned) glass over ice and garnish. Or screw the garnish and just knock it back. This is another case where you can float some overproof rum on top, betraying yourself for what you really are which is little better than a common rummy.

9) JUAN COLLINS

3 oz. light rum
1 oz. lemon juice
1-2 tsp. sugar
club soda
orange slice, lemon slice & maraschino
cherry garnish

The classic Tom Collins with a Caribbean twist. Mix rum, juice and sugar
over ice in a shaker. Strain into tall -
you guessed it - tom collins glass 1/2
filled with ice and top with soda. The
fruit garnish is optional, but does add
a festive touch. So make the
effort ya' slug.

10) MINT RUMLEP

3 oz. golden or dark rum
15 mint leaves
1 tsp. sugar
2 tsp. water

The classic mint julep made with rum.
Tear 10 mint leaves in half and muddle
(mash) in a tall (tom collins) glass with
sugar and water. Half fill the glass
with cracked ice and add rum. Toss in
the rest of the mint and top off with
cracked ice. The Booze Fairy recommends using a straw so you don't get
mint in your teeth. And, of course, the
stronger the rum the better the julep.

Tutti Frutti

TUTTI FRUTTI

Rum and fruit go together like well...
tutti and frutti. The sweet smoothness of a fine rum mixes perfectly
with all manner of fruit juices – from
sweet to tart. The fruit also mellows
the booze bite so these cocktails are
the perfect candidates for strong and
overproof rums. In fact they're so
smooth it's easy to forget how potent
they are. The Booze Fairy advises
you to take your time standing up before you go mix yourself another.

1) PLANTER'S PUNCH

3 oz. dark rum
3 oz. orange juice
1 oz. lemon juice
1/2 tsp. grenadine
1 tsp. sugar
orange & lemon slice garnishes

Mix all ingredients over ice in a shaker. Strain into a tall (tom collins) glass 1/2 filled with ice, adding ice if necessary to fill it then garnish. According to the Booze Fairy this cocktail got its name because after one or two you're pretty firmly planted.

2) APRICOT LADY

2 oz. light rum
1 oz. apricot brandy
1 tsp. orange curaçao
1 tsp. lime juice
orange slice garnish

Crush enough ice in a blender to make 1/2 cup. Add ingredients and blend at low speed 10-15 seconds. Pour into a short (old-fashioned) glass, float orange slice on top and drink up. If you like yours frothier, and protein rich, add a little egg white when blending. Your pecs and glutes will thank you.

3) BANANA MANGO TANGO

2 oz. light rum
1/2 oz. banana liqueur
1/2 oz. mango nectar
1/2 oz. lime juice
mango slice garnish

Mix all ingredients over ice in shaker.
Strain into a short (old-fashioned)
glass, or plastic cup if you're under
50, add 2 or 3 ice cubes and garnish
with mango slice. This cocktail an-
swers the age-old question one con-
fronts when you encounter mangoes
at the grocery store - what the heck
are these good for? Now you know!

4) BITTER BANANA COOLER

2 oz. light rum
1/4 cup banana slices
1/4 cup pineapple juice
1/2 oz. lime juice
2 dashes Peychaud's (or Angostura)
bitters
bitter lemon soda

Crush enough ice in a blender to
make 1/2 cup. Add rum, banana slices,
juices, more rum and bitters. Blend at
high speed 10-15 seconds. Pour into
a tall (tom collins) glass with a few ice
cubes and top with bitter lemon soda.
To quote Socrates, sometimes bitter
is better. And hold the hemlock.

5) BLUEBERRY RUM FIZZ

3 oz. light rum
1 tsp. triple sec
1/2 oz. blueberry syrup
1 tbsp. lemon juice
club soda
lemon slice & 2-3 blueberries garnish

Mix rum, triple sec, syrup and lemon juice over ice in a shaker. Strain into a tall (tom collins) glass 1/2 filled with ice, top off with club soda, drop in the berries and float the lemon slice. Now you know what to do with blueberries when they're in season, or even when they're not.

6) CRANBERRY RUM PUNCH

2 oz. light rum
1 oz. dark rum
4 oz. cranberry juice
2 oz. orange juice
1/2 oz. lemon juice
lemon slice garnish

Mix rums and juices over ice in a shaker. Strain into a tall (tom collins) glass 1/2 filled with ice and garnish with lemon slice. The Booze Fairy thinks you'll find this is a much, much better use for cranberries than that awful canned "sauce" at Thanksgiving.

7) FERN GULLY FIZZ

2 oz. light rum
1 oz. dark rum
1 oz. pineapple juice
1/2 oz. lime juice
1 tsp. sugar
club soda
lime slice & pineapple slice (or chunk)
garnish

Mix rum, juice and sugar over ice in a shaker. Strain into a tall (tom collins) glass 1/2 filled with ice, top off with soda and garnish. If you must watch a certain sappy animated movie by the same name, a few of these might just get you through it.

8) ORANGE COLADA

2 oz. light rum
1 oz. dark rum
4 oz. orange juice
1 oz. coconut cream, or coconut milk
1 tsp. sugar

Crush enough ice in a blender to make 1/2 cup. Add ingredients and blend at high speed for 10-15 seconds. Pour into a tall (tom collins) glass with a few ice cubes. Basically a piña colada with orange juice instead of pineapple. The O.J makes it perfect for breakfast.

9) PASSION FRUIT COOLER

3 oz. light rum
4 oz. passion fruit nectar (not syrup)
1 oz. orange juice
1/2 oz. lemon juice
2 sprigs mint garnish

Mix rum, nectar and juice over ice in a shaker. Strain into a tall (tom collins) glass with a few ice cubes. Tear the mint sprig garnish to release the fragrance. The Booze Fairy also likes to swab his pits with mint when he's not feeling fresh. Hey, don't knock it till you've tried it pal.

10) WATERMELON COOLER

3 oz. light rum
1/2 oz. maraschino cherry liqueur
1/2 cup diced watermelon (no seeds
please)
1/2 oz. lime juice
1 tsp. sugar
lime slice garnish

Crush enough ice in a blender to
make 1/2 cup. Add ingredients and
blend at low speed for 10-15 seconds.
Pour in a tall (tom collins) glass with a
few ice cubes and garnish. Watermelon, it's not just for vodka
infusions any more!

DAIQUIRI DAIQUIRI DOCK

The daiquiri, one of the Booze Fairy's Top Ten Classics, is named for the Cuban beach where it was born over 100 years ago. Originally stirred over ice in a tall glass, soon daiquiris were being shaken with shaved ice. From there it was a short trip to the blender to create the frozen favorite, often with some kind of fruit added. The daiquiri is nothing if not versatile and an excellent delivery device for overproof rum and was a breakfast favorite of Papa Hemingway. If you don't see your favorite rum or fruit in these recipes the Booze Fairy encourages you to experiment in the name of booze science!

1) FROZEN DAIQUIRI

3 oz. light or golden rum
1 oz. lime juice
1 tsp. sugar, or simple syrup
1 tsp. overproof rum to float
(optional)

Crush enough ice in a blender to make 1/2 cup. Add all ingredients and blend at low speed for 10-15 seconds. Pour into a martini or champagne glass or chug straight from the blender. Floating a bit of overproof rum will make the Booze Fairy proud. And isn't it about time you did something for you?

2) FLORIDITA

2 oz. light or golden rum
1/2 oz. lime juice
1 oz. maraschino cherry liqueur
1 tsp. sugar (or simple syrup)

Mix all ingredients in a shaker over ice.
Strain into a martini or champagne
glass to show you're classy. The
Floridita is also known as the Hemingway Daiquiri because, like the Booze
Fairy, Papa H had to tinker with
his cocktails.

3) CHERRY DAIQUIRI

2 oz. light or golden rum
1/2 oz. lime juice
1 oz. cherry liqueur
1/2 tsp. kirschwasser (clear cherry
brandy)
lime peel garnish

Mix all ingredients over ice in a shaker. Strain into a martini or champagne glass, twist lime peel juice into drink and drop in. If this cherry concoction doesn't make you cheery,
add more rum.

4) DERBY DAIQUIRI

2 oz. light rum
1/2 oz. lime juice
1 oz. orange juice
1/2 oz. simple syrup

Crush enough ice in a blender to make 1/2 cup. Add all ingredients and blend at low speed for 10-15 seconds. Pour into a martini or champagne glass. Of course, if you serve it in a little plastic derby it'll save you the trouble of telling people what it's called.

5) FROZEN STRAWBERRY DAIQUIRI

2 oz. light rum
1/2 oz. lime juice
1/4 cup thawed frozen strawberries in syrup
1 tsp. maraschino cherry liqueur
1 tsp sugar or simple syrup
1/2 oz. heavy cream

Crush enough ice in a blender to make 1/2 cup. Add all ingredients and blend at high speed for 10-15 seconds. Pour into a martini or champagne glass. You can also make these with fresh strawberries, but why bother? They're just gonna get frozen anyway.

6) FROZEN APPLE DAIQUIRI

2 oz. light rum
1/2 oz. lemon juice
1/2 oz. apple juice
1 tsp. sugar or simple syrup
apple wedge with skin garnish

Crush enough ice in a blender to make 1/2 cup. Add all ingredients and blend at low speed for 10-15 seconds. Pour into martini or champagne glass and garnish with apple wedge. Back when he was a boy, the Booze Fairy always brought his teacher one of these for the first day of school. He graduated with honors and a wicked hangover.

7) BANANA DAIQUIRI

2 oz. light rum
1 oz. banana liqueur
1 oz. orange juice
1/2 oz. lemon juice

Crush enough ice in blender to make
1/2 cup. Add all ingredients and blend
at high speed for 10-15 seconds. Pour
into a martini or champagne glass.
You can also make this using 1/2 a ripe
banana sliced instead of the liqueur.
At last, something to do with that
overripe banana blackening on your
kitchen counter.

8) FROZEN MINT DAIQUIRI

2 oz. light rum
1/2 oz lemon juice
1 tsp. sugar, or simple syrup
6 large mint leaves

Crush enough ice in a blender to make 1/2 cup. Add all ingredients and blend at low speed for 20 seconds. Pour into a martini or champagne glass. The Booze Fairy prefers spearmint, but the kind of mint is up to you. It's your cocktail after all, dammit!

9) FROZEN PASSION FRUIT DAIQUIRI

2 oz. light rum
1/2 oz. lime juice
1/2 oz. passion fruit syrup (not nectar)
1/2 oz. orange juice
1/2 oz. lemon juice

Crush enough ice in a blender to make 1/2 cup. Add all ingredients and blend at low speed for 10-15 seconds. Pour into a martini or champagne glass. At last, something to do with all that passion fruit syrup you have lying around.

10) FROZEN PEACH DAIQUIRI

2 oz. light rum
1/2 oz lime juice
1/2 cup thawed frozen peaches with
syrup

Crush enough ice in a blender to
make 1/2 cup. Add all ingredients and
blend at low speed for 10-15 seconds.
Pour into a martini or champagne
glass. On a hot summer day it makes a
"peach" of a cocktail. Hey, these little
quips can't all be LOL!

TIKI TIME

There are no hard and fast rules for what makes a cocktail "tiki" but the Booze Fairy, scholar of all things intoxicating, has identified four common elements. 1) Buttloads of rum. 2) Tropical fruits and juices. 3) Spices - both spiced rums and on their own. And most importantly, 4) Tiki presentation. So be creative boys and girls. Break out the exotic fruit juices, hollowed out pineapples, coconut shells, swizzle sticks, tiki glasses, mugs and totems, fruit garnishes, edible flowers and, of course, the little paper umbrellas and plastic monkeys. Then light the torches and start the luau. It's Tiki Time!

1) RUM-APOR SLING

2 oz. light rum
1 oz. cherry brandy or liqueur
1 oz. herbal liqueur (like Benedictine)
2 oz. pineapple juice
squeeze of lime wedge
dash of Angostura bitters
club soda
orange slice & maraschino cherry

Mix all ingredients except soda in a shaker over ice. Strain into a tiki-worthy container of your choice. Top with club soda. Garnish with orange slice and cherry then follow the Booze Fairy to the conga line!

2) TIKARITA

2 oz. spiced rum
1/2 oz. pineapple juice
1/2 oz. triple sec
1/2 oz. lime juice
maraschino cherry & lime wedge garnish

Crush enough ice in a blender to make
1/2 cup. Add rum, triple sec and juices
and blend at high speed for 10-15 seconds till smooth. Pour into a tiki-worthy
container. Garnish with cherry and lime.
Tiny umbrella and little plastic
monkey (optional).

3) PAIN KILLER

2 oz. dark or Navy rum
4 oz. pineapple juice
1 oz. cream of coconut
1 oz. orange juice
fresh grated nutmeg
pineapple wedge garnish

Mix rum and juices in a shaker over ice. Pour into a tiki-worthy container then sprinkle with nutmeg, garnish with pineapple, and let this fine concoction make the pain go away.

4) TIKI TORCH

2 oz. light rum
1 oz. orange juice
1 oz. lime juice
1 oz. grenadine
1/2 oz. pineapple syrup
dash of Angostura bitters
lemon half, hollowed
1/2 oz. overproof rum to float and ignite

Mix light rum, juices and pineapple syrup in a shaker over ice. Pour grenadine into a ti-ki-worthy container over ice. Slowly strain in rum/juice/syrup mix and a dash of bitters. Pour overproof rum into lemon half, float it on top and ignite it with a fireplace match or bbq grill lighter. CAUTION! - please dear lord wait for the fire to go out before consuming. The singed eyebrow look is so last year.

5) TANGERINE TIKI

2 oz. golden or aged rum
2 oz. tangerine juice
1 oz. pineapple juice
1 oz. lime juice
dash coconut or Angostura bitters
pineapple & orange slice

Mix rum, juices and bitters in a shaker over ice. Pour into a tiki-worthy container over ice, garnish with fruit slices and enjoy. Then mix another one and enjoy again. Keep enjoying till you're all enjoyed out.

6) BIRD OF PARADISE

2 oz. dark rum
1 oz. Campari
1/2 oz. simple syrup
2 oz. pineapple juice
1/2 oz. lime juice
pineapple wedge garnish

Mix rum, Campari, syrup and juice in a shaker over ice. Pour into a tiki-worthy container over ice. Garnish with pineapple and fly away to the tropical paradise of your dreams.

7) TIKI COCO LOCO

2 oz. coconut rum
2 oz. light rum
1/2 oz. hazelnut liqueur
2 oz. cream of coconut
3 oz. mango nectar
1/4 banana
1/2 oz. dark rum to float
1 tbsp. shredded coconut
whipped cream

Crush enough ice in a blender to make 1/2 cup. Add coconut and light rums, hazelnut liqueur, cream of coconut, mango nectar and banana. Blend at high speed for 10-15 seconds until smooth. Pour into a tiki-worthy container (preferably a half coconut) and float dark rum. Topped with shredded coconut and whipped cream, it's a liquid desert island dessert!

8) FREAKI TIKI

1 oz. spiced rum
1 oz. coconut rum
2 oz. cranberry juice
1 oz. orange juice
1/2 oz. simple syrup
1/2 oz. lemon juice
club soda
lime wedge garnish

Mix rum, juice and syrup in a tiki-worthy container over ice. Stir well. Top
with club soda and garnish with lime
wedge. Prepare to get freaky
tiki deeky.

9) TIKI RUM PUNCH

2 oz. light rum
1 oz. pineapple juice
1 oz. orange juice
1 oz. grapefruit juice
1/2 oz. grenadine
club soda
lime wedge
pineapple, cherries, oranges
& lime pieces for garnish

Mix rum, fruit juices, grenadine and squeeze of lime wedge into a shaker over ice. Fill a tiki-worthy container with ice, add a splash of soda and strain in the punch. Garnish liberally with fruit pieces. If you're feeling a bit naughty use overproof rum, put on some Barry White and let the magic happen.

10) MY BLUE TIKI

2 oz. light rum
1 oz. lemon juice
1 oz. pineapple juice
1 oz. blue curaçao
1 oz. honey
1 oz. Amaretto
mint for muddling and garnish
little umbrella (mandatory)

Mix all ingredients except mint over
ice in a shaker. Muddle (mash) a few
mint leaves in a tall tiki-worthy container - preferably clear so you can
enjoy its color - and fill with ice. Strain
in cocktail and garnish with mint. It's
the tiki way to kick the blues.

HOLIDAY CHEER

Towards the end of November, as the holidays loom and temperatures turn nippy, rum takes on a whole new persona. Now it's a warm, comforting friend that helps you tolerate both the crappy weather and your relatives. It's a welcome presence not just in festive cocktails and warm toddies, but also in holiday confections like rum balls and fruitcake which it actually makes edible. So come that magical time of year you owe it to yourself to enjoy a little holiday cheer whether you've been naughty, nice or somewhere on the spectrum in between.

1) RUMNOG

2 oz. dark rum
6 oz. milk
1 tsp. powdered sugar
1 egg yolk
freshly grated nutmeg

Mix rum, milk, sugar and egg yolk over
ice in a shaker. Strain into a tall (tom
collins) glass 1/2 filled with ice and top
with freshly ground nutmeg to taste.
Then taste, taste, taste! The nutmeg
marries the richness of the egg to
the aromatics of the rum. The Booze
Fairy usually just buys pre-made egg-
nog and spikes it. But he never ever
skips, or scrimps on, the fresh nutmeg. It's the key to this cocktail!

2) RUM TODDY

3 oz. golden or dark rum
1 tsp. sugar
3 whole cloves
1 cinnamon stick
1 lemon slice
boiling water
fresh ground nutmeg for garnish

Put sugar, cloves, cinnamon and lemon slice into a coffee mug. Add 1-2 oz. boiling water and mix well. Let it stand for 5 minutes so the hot water can marry the flavors. Add the rum and enough boiling water to fill the mug. Sprinkle with ground nutmeg to taste. On a cold, winter's day there's nothing like a hot toddy to warm the cockles of your heart, whatever the heck cockles are.

3) HOT BUTTERED RUM

2 oz. light rum
1 oz. dark rum
2 whole cloves
2 allspice berries
1 cinnamon stick
1 tsp. sugar
1 tsp. butter
boiling water

A lo-cal treat! Put spices and sugar in a coffee mug and add 1-2 oz. boiling water. Let it stand for 5 minutes so the hot water can marry the flavors. Add rum, butter and enough boiling water to fill the mug. Stir until butter dissolves. You can also cut to the chase and simply use golden rum, or go crazy and use spiced rum. Hey, it's your cocktail. Have it your way.

4) MULLED RUM

2 oz. golden or dark rum
1 oz. Drambuie
2 dashes Angostura bitters
lemon peel
boiling water
maraschino cherry garnish

Pour rum, Drambuie and bitters into
a coffee mug, add lemon peel and fill
with boiling water. Add cherry. Don't
bother mulling it over. Just enjoy!

5) CAFÉ CUBANO FUERTE

2 oz. dark rum
1 oz. heavy cream
2 tsp. sugar
hot café Cubano

Prepare a pot of strong Cuban
espresso. In a small bowl whisk cream,
sugar and 1 tbsp. of the hot coffee to
make a foamy crema. Pour rum into
a coffee mug and 1/2 fill with coffee.
Spoon crema on top. Mixing a strong
coffee buzz with a nice rum kick, it's
it's the perfect way to face all those
awful holiday chores.

6) RUM & JERRY

1 oz. dark rum
1 oz. brandy
4 oz. hot milk or water
1 tbsp. Tom & Jerry batter
fresh ground nutmeg

Add rum, brandy and Tom & Jerry batter to a coffee mug or cup. Stir in hot milk, or water (or a mixture of the two) until the drink is foamy. Garnish with nutmeg.

Okay, okay… so T&J batter is widely available in liquor and grocery stores during the holidays. But what if you're a purest and want to make your own? Knock yourself out, Sparky. The ingredients are…

12 eggs (separated)
1 tsp. cream of tartar
1/2 cup (1 stick) softened butter
1 cup sugar
1 tsp. ground cinnamon
1 tsp. ground cloves
1 tsp. ground nutmeg
1 tsp. vanilla extract
2 oz. dark rum

Still interested? Okee-dokey. Separate egg whites and yolks into two mixing bowls. Add cream of tartar to the whites and whip with a hand mixer into a meringue with stiff peaks. Whisk the softened butter and sugar into the yolks. Gently fold yolk mixture into the egg white meringue. Stir in spices, vanilla and rum. Voilà! You have homemade Tom & Jerry batter to store in your fridge until needed. FYI ~ even the Booze Fairy wouldn't go through this brain damage for a simple cocktail, and he's one committed boozer.

7) RUM CHOCOLATE

1 oz. golden rum
1 oz. crème de cacao
1 tbsp. heavy cream, or half & half
hot chocolate
marshmallow garnish

Pour rum, crème de cacao and cream into a coffee mug. Fill with your favorite hot chocolate. Float in a marshmallow, or two. Think of it as a booze-infused cold weather treat for both your inner rummy and chocolate-loving inner child.

8) RUM SPARKLER

2 oz. dark rum
1 oz. apple juice
chilled champagne or
sparkling white wine
1 oz. honey
2 oz. hot water
apple slice & mint sprig garnish

In a small bowl mix honey and hot water. Stir until honey dissolves. NOTE:
This is enough honey syrup for 6
drinks. Mix rum, apple juice and 1/2
oz. syrup over ice in a shaker. Strain
into a short (old-fashioned) glass
filled with ice. Top with champagne
and garnish. This festive cocktail will
definitely take your holiday entertain-
ing from ho-hum to fabulous in the
blink of an eye.

9) SPICED RUM CIDER

1 cup dark rum
2 qt. apple cider
1 orange thinly sliced
1 apple halved
1/2 cup brown sugar
2 tsp. whole cloves
1 tsp. allspice
pinch of fresh grated nutmeg
cinnamon sticks for garnish

This is a batch cocktail that makes 8 servings. In a large pot simmer cider, apple, orange and spices over low heat for 15 minutes. Remove from heat, discard fruit and add rum. Ladle into mugs. Garnish with a cinnamon stick. It's a drink to savor in your warm, comfy home while Christmas carolers freeze their hineys off outside.

10) HOLIDAY RUM MULE

3 oz. dark rum
1/2 oz. lime juice
ginger beer
lime wedges & whole fresh cranberries for garnish

Mix rum and lime juice over ice in a
shaker. Strain into a tall (tom collins)
glass with a few ice cubes then top
with ginger beer until about 2/3 full.
Add lime wedge and 3-4 cranberries
for garnish and flavor. Substitute 1 oz.
overproof rum for some of the dark
rum and this mule will really kick.

NICE N' SPICEY

Who doesn't enjoy spicing things up a bit? Well that's exactly what the Booze Fairy has been inspiring folks to do with rum since forever, adding all manner of spices and herbs to the already flavorful liquor. While spiced rums are perfectly fine on their own - perhaps on the rocks garnished with an orange slice and/or a cinnamon stick - they're also a great mixer. And though most of us prefer to simply buy ours, the Booze Fairy enjoys making his own. His recipe starts off the list.

1) THE BOOZE FAIRY'S SPICED RUM

1 bottle golden rum
1 split vanilla bean
3 whole cloves
1 cinnamon stick
3 allspice berries
1 piece star anise
1/8 tsp fresh-grated nutmeg
1 pinch of fairy dust (or 1 tsp. sugar)

Combine everything in a large jar or jug and seal. Refrigerate for 4 days, shaking once a day to mix the ingredients. After 4 days strain rum back into the bottle. While his recipe is tried and true, the Booze Fairy encourages you to create your own spice combinations, adding and subtracting ingredients from his recipe with things like citrus zest, cardamom pods, fresh ginger slices or even whole peppercorns.

2) ALOHA COLLINS

4 oz. spiced rum
2 oz. lemon juice
2 oz. guava juice
lemon slice & maraschino cherry garnish

Mix rum and juices over ice in a shaker. Strain into a tall (tom collins) glass
1/2 filled with ice. Garnish with lemon
and cherry then say "aloha" to the
stresses and strains of your hectic
life. Feel free to put on a grass skirt
and hula the day away.

3) CABLE CAR

3 oz. spiced rum
1/2 oz. lemon juice
1 tsp. orange juice
1 tsp. sugar or simple syrup
orange slice garnish
1 tsp. overproof rum to float (optional)

Mix rum, juices and sugar over ice in a
shaker. Strain into a short (old-fashioned) glass and garnish. If you want
a little something extra, float a tsp.
of overproof rum on top. Anyway
you slice it, this is one form of pub-
lic transportation the Booze Fairy is
more than happy to climb aboard.

4) BLACKBEARD

2 oz. spiced rum
2 oz. root beer schnapps
your favorite root beer, or birch beer

Pour rum and schnapps over ice in a
short (old-fashioned) glass. Top off
with root beer. Not sure if the infa-
mous pirate ever carried any root
beer or schnapps on board, but he
darn sure had a buttload of rum and
would certainly be pleased as punch
to have this fine libation named
after him.

5) SPICY RUM MULE

3 oz. spiced rum
ginger beer
lime wedge garnish

Pour rum into a short (old-fashioned)
glass filled with ice and top with ginger
beer. Squeeze lime wedge into cocktail and float as garnish. Substitute
1 oz. overproof rum for 1 oz. of the
spiced rum if you like your mule a little
more "stubborn."

6) SPICY RUM SHARK

2 oz. spiced rum
2 oz. blue curaçao
3 oz. pineapple juice
ginger beer
maraschino cherry garnish

Mix rum, curaçao and juice over ice in a shaker. Strain into a tall (tom collins) glass filled with ice, top off with ginger beer and garnish with cherry. If the spice in the rum doesn't get your attention the Day-Glo blue green color will.

7) SPICE-CAPADES

3 oz. spiced rum
1 oz. guava nectar (not syrup)
1/2 oz. lime juice
1 tsp. banana liqueur

Crush enough ice in a blender to make 1/2 cup. Blend all ingredients on low speed for 10-15 seconds. Pour into a martini or champagne glass. This spiced up twist on a tropical frozen daiquiri will make you glad you finally sprung for that blender ya' tightwad.

8) FULL MOON FEVER

2 oz. spiced rum
1 oz. light rum
1 oz. coconut rum
1 oz. melon liqueur
3 oz. pineapple juice
1 oz. Rose's lime juice

Mix all ingredients over ice in a shaker. Strain into a tall (tom collins) glass 1/2 filled with ice. They say the full moon drives people mad. While this cocktail won't do that, it'll definitely drive you waaaaaayyy around the bend.

9) SUNRISE BAHAMA MAMA

2 oz. spiced rum
1 oz. dark rum
4 oz. orange juice
2 oz. pineapple juice
1/2 oz. grenadine
maraschino cherry garnish

Mix rum and juices over ice in a shaker. Strain into a tall (tom collins) glass 1/2 filled with ice. Float grenadine on top and garnish with cherry. Start drinking these at sunset and you ain't gonna see the sunrise, at least not standing up.

10) TSUNAMI

2 oz. spiced rum
1 oz. coconut rum
1 oz. dark rum
4 oz. pineapple juice
1 tsp. grenadine

Mix rum and juice over ice in a shaker. Strain into a tall (tom collins) glass filled with ice and float grenadine on top. This tsunami won't just blow you away. It'll pick you up and drop you three islands over.

RUM RUNNERS

Many years ago America went seriously off the rails and made booze illegal. As the Booze Fairy is fond of saying "the road to Hell is paved with dumb ideas," and the "noble experiment" known as Prohibition was perhaps the dumbest idea ever until the invention of the mullet. No sooner was hooch illegal than freedom-loving Americans found other ways to get it. The era gave rise to bootleggers, speakeasies and rum runners, valiant souls who braved the Coast Guard at sea and law enforcement on shore to provide the vital elixir. As you enjoy these Roaring Twenties cocktails, take a moment to salute the heroes who made them possible for our forebears those many years ago.

1) RUM HIGHBALL

3 oz. golden or dark rum
club soda, sweet soda or ginger ale
lime slice garnish

Pour rum into a tall (tom collins) glass
filled with ice. Top off with your soda of
choice and garnish with lime slice. Booze
with a spritz ~ what could be simpler? And
as the Booze Fairy is fond of saying, the
better the rum the better the highball. But
you didn't need a drunken fairy to tell you
that, now did you?

2) BEE'S KNEES

3 oz. light or golden rum
1/2 oz. orange juice
1/2 oz. lime juice
tsp. sugar or simple syrup
2 dashes orange bitters
orange peel garnish

Mix rum, juice, sugar and bitters over
ice in a shaker. Strain into a short
(old-fashioned) glass, twist peel juice
into drink and then drop it in. This
was a speakeasy favorite with distinct
orange flair, or in the lingo of the day
"it's the bee's knees."

3) RUM SIDECAR

2 oz. golden rum
1/2 oz. orange liqueur
1/2 oz. lemon juice
1 oz. dark rum to float

Mix golden rum, orange liqueur and lemon juice over ice in a shaker. Strain into short (old-fashioned) glass filled with ice. Float dark rum on top. This cocktail was invented near the end of WWI and was named for the then popular motorcycle sidecar attachment. Why? Who the heck knows? Just enjoy the ride.

4) RABBIT'S FOOT

3 oz. light rum
1 oz. apple juice
1 oz. orange juice
1/2 oz. lemon juice
1/2 oz. grenadine
orange slice garnish

Mix rum, juices and grenadine over
ice in a shaker. Strain into a short
(old-fashioned) glass fill with ice and
garnish with orange slice. A rabbit's
foot is considered a good luck charm,
but how do you think the rabbit
feels about it?

5) RUM RICKEY

3 oz. light, golden or dark rum
club soda
lime peel garnish

Pour rum into a short (old-fashioned)
glass filled with ice and top with soda.
Twist lime peel juice into the cocktail and
then drop it in. This drink shot to fame in
Washington, D.C. at the turn of the 20th
century. Originally made with bourbon
then gin, once Prohibition hit folks got a
bit more open minded about what kind of
booze to make it with.

6) MARY PICKFORD

3 oz. light rum
1 tsp. maraschino cherry liqueur
1 tsp. grenadine
1 oz. pineapple juice
maraschino cherry garnish

Mix rum, liqueur, grenadine and juice over ice in a shaker. Strain into a champagne or martini glass and garnish with cherry. Named for America's Sweetheart, silent movie star Mary Pickford, it has the quiet grace of a bygone era. And like a movie star getting ready for a closeup you will get properly lit.

7) RUM STINGER

2 oz. overproof rum
2 oz. amaretto
your favorite cola

Pour rum and amaretto into a tall (tom collins) glass filled with ice and top off with
cola. Sip this one slowly and you'll still feel
its sting ~ and that ain't such a bad thing.
Fun Fact: during Prohibition instead of
amaretto, stingers were usually made with
crème de menthe to mask the taste of the
rotgut booze that was often served.

8) SHANGHAI COCKTAIL

3 oz. light rum
1 oz. anisette
1 tsp. grenadine
1/2 oz lemon juice

Mix all ingredients over ice in a shaker. Strain into a martini or champagne glass, and prepare to have your senses shanghaied - which is to say clubbed, drugged and dragged aboard a strange ship to an unknown destination just like in the good old days.

9) RUM BUCK

3 oz. light rum
1/2 oz. lime juice
dash of Angostura bitters
ginger ale
almond slivers & lime slice garnish

Mix rum, lime juice and bitters over ice in a shaker. Strain into a tall (tom collins) glass 1/2 filled with ice and top with ginger ale. Sprinkle almond slivers on top and garnish with lime. It's also known as the Barbados Buck or Jamaican Buck, depending on the source of the rum. The Booze Fairy calls his the Discount Liquor Store Buck.

10) SHORE LEAVE

2 oz. light rum
1 oz. sloe gin
1/2 oz. lime juice
tonic water
lime slice garnish

Mix rum, sloe gin and juice over ice in
a shaker. Strain into a tall (tom collins) glass 1/2 filled with ice. Top off
with tonic water and garnish with lime.
A more flavorful take on the gin and
tonic, it's a fine way to take your leave
at the end of a long, hot day.

ISLAND DELIGHTS

ISLAND DELIGHTS

The mojito is perhaps the most famous rum cocktail associated with
the Caribbean islands. A refreshing
combination of rum, sugar, lime and
mint, the mojito is one of the Booze
Fairy's Top Ten Classics. More than
any other spirit, rum is associated
with the dream of an idyllic island life
of soft tropical breezes, gently sway-
ing palm trees and clothing-optional
romps on white sand beaches. And
as the names of these cocktails con-
jure up island images, the Booze Fairy
believes these drinks will transport
you away from your dull, drab, dreary
day. By which, of course, he means
they will get you really, really stinky.

1) BLUE HAWAII

2 oz. light rum
2 oz. blue curaçao
3 oz. pineapple juice
1 oz. cream of coconut, or coconut milk
pineapple chunk & maraschino cherry garnish

Mix all ingredients over ice in a shaker. Strain into tall (tom collins) glass and garnish. It can also be served frozen by crushing enough ice in a blender to make 1/2 a cup and blending all the ingredients on high speed for 10-15 seconds. Your choice. It's nice to have choices, right?

2) JAMAICAN GINGER

2 oz. light rum
1 oz. dark rum
1/2 oz overproof rum
1/2 oz. Falernum, or spiced rum
1/2 oz. lime juice
1 tsp. fresh grated ginger
ginger beer
pineapple chunk garnish

Mix rums, Falernum (Google it, dude),
lime juice and grated ginger over ice in
a shaker. Strain into a tall (tom collins) glass 1/2 filled with ice. Top off
with ginger beer and garnish. With
that much ginger perhaps this cocktail
should be called the Rum Redhead.

3) CUBA LIBRE

3 oz. golden or dark rum
2 lime wedges
your favorite cola
1/2 tsp. overproof rum to float (optional)

Pour rum into a tall (tom collins) glass
1/2 filled with ice. Squeeze lime wedges
into rum and drop into drink. Top off
with cola and float the overproof rum
on top if desired. Okay, so it's basically a very limey rum and cola but it
does have an island name. Fire up a
fine Cuban cigar and imagine you're
hiding in the jungle with Fidel and Che
waiting for the perfect moment to
liberate the island.

4) BAHAMA MAMA

1 oz. dark rum
1/2 oz. coconut liqueur
1/2 oz. coffee liqueur
1/2 oz. overproof rum
4 oz. pineapple juice
1/2 oz lemon juice
pineapple chunk garnish

Mix rum, liqueurs and juice over ice in a shaker. Strain into a tall (tom collins) glass 1/2 filled with ice and garnish. BTW - the runner-up name for this cocktail was Bahama Papa, but it just didn't have the same ring to it.

5) BEACHCOMBER

2 oz. light rum
1/2 oz. lime juice
1/2 oz. triple sec
1/2 tsp. maraschino cherry liqueur
sugar for rimming glass

Mix all ingredients over ice in a shaker. Strain into a martini or champagne glass rimmed with sugar and sip, sip, sip! This concoction goes down easy… too easy. You should also note that beachcombers don't actually comb the beach. They just sort of hang out.

6) CARIBBEAN PUNCH

2 oz. light rum
1 oz. dark rum
1/2 oz banana liqueur
2 oz. pineapple juice
2 oz. orange juice
1/2 oz. lime juice

Mix all ingredients over ice in a shaker.
Strain into a tall (tom collins) glass 1/2
filled with ice. If you think about it you
could split the difference rum-wise
and go with 3 oz. of golden rum and
pretty much get to the same flavor.
Just don't overthink it.

7) GUAGIN

3 oz. light rum
1 oz. passion fruit syrup (not nectar)
1/2 oz. lemon juice
1/2 oz. lime juice
maraschino cherry garnish

Crush enough ice in a blender to make 1/2 cup. Add all ingredients and blend at low speed for 10-15 seconds. Pour into a martini or champagne glass and garnish. Legend has it this cocktail is why Gaugin's paintings went all primitive once he hit Tahiti. Or maybe it was the syphilis. We'll really never know, will we?

8) PAGO PAGO

2 oz. golden rum
1/2 oz. lime juice
1/2 oz. pineapple juice
1/2 tsp. green Chartreuse
1/2 tsp. white crème de cacao

Mix all ingredients over ice in a shaker. Strain into a martini or champagne glass. In case you're wondering, Pago Pago is the capital of American Samoa. Who the heck knows why it has its own cocktail. The Booze Fairy thinks the name Samoan Slammer would be more kick-ass.

9) ST. CROIX COOLER

2 oz. light rum
1 oz. dark rum
1 oz. brandy
1 tbsp. brown sugar
3 oz. orange juice
1 oz. lemon juice
dash of orange bitters
club soda
large orange peel

Mix rum, brandy, sugar, bitters and juices over ice in a shaker. Strain into a tall (tom collins) glass 1/2 filled with ice, add orange peel and top off with soda. St. Croix is one of the U.S. Virgin Islands. You have to wonder, if they're drinking these on a regular basis just how many virgins are left.

10) TAHITI CLUB

3 oz. golden rum
1/2 oz lime juice
1/2 oz. pineapple juice
1 tsp. maraschino cherry liqueur
orange slice garnish

Mix rum, juice and liqueur over ice in a shaker. Strain into a short (old-fashioned) glass filled with ice and garnish. The Booze Fairy thinks it's called the Tahiti Club because it hits you in the head like a club. But you're in Tahiti so who cares?!

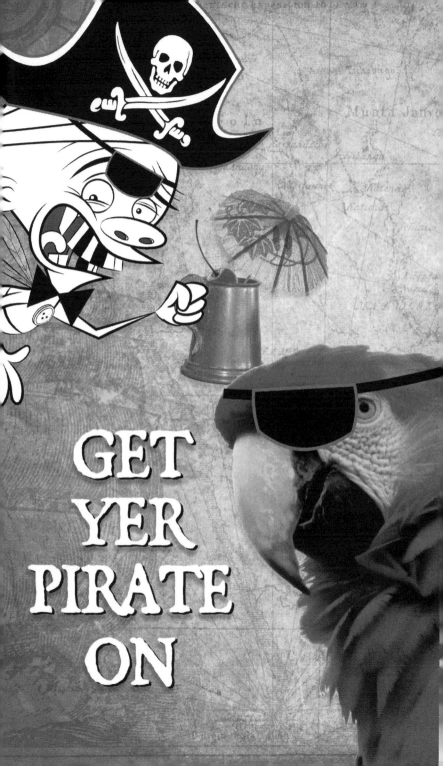

Get Your Pirate On

When it comes to cocktail recipes the Booze Fairy's gotta get in his two cents in like the opinionated, loud-mouth drunk he is. So with visions of pirates dancing in his booze-soaked brain he came up with his own con-coctions for a pirate-themed party he's gonna throw one of these days. Needless to say all bets are off if you wanna try 'em. Who knows? You might even enjoy 'em. Even a broken com-pass is right if you happen to be sail-ing in the right direction in the first place.

1) PEG LEG PIÑA

2 oz. light rum
3 oz. mango or jackfruit juice
1 oz. coconut cream, or coconut milk
cinnamon stick garnish

Gently mix rum, juice and coconut cream (or milk) in a shaker with crushed ice. Pour into a short (old-fashioned) glass and garnish with a cinnamon stick peg leg. The Booze Fairy also prepares a "frozen" variety by crushing 1/2 cup ice in the blender, adding the ingredients and blending at low speed for 10-15 seconds. Because the crushed ice waters things down in his opinion, he usually substitutes overproof rum.

2) JOLLY RUM-GER

3 oz. light rum
2 oz. pineapple juice
2 oz. orange juice
1 oz grenadine
your favorite fruit gummies garnish

Mix rum, juice and grenadine over ice in a shaker. Strain into a tall (tom collins) glass 1/2 filled with ice. Garnish liberally with your favorite fruit gummies. Totally optional - but totally awesome - if you're feeling creative make a little skull and crossbones Jolly Roger flag to fly proudly over your cocktail.

3) DRUNKEN TREASURE

1 shot glass of overproof rum
1 tankard India pale ale

A pirate riff on the classic Depth Charge. Fill your sturdy tankard (mug, stein, Mason jar) 2/3 with ale (or your favorite beer), "sink" the shot of rum and swill it down like the filthy brigand you are. The Booze Fairy recommends keeping an eye on how far you tilt the tankard. That shot glass can slide, and he's lost a couple teeth that way. While an eye patch can make you look dashing, a missing tooth just makes you look dumb.

4) RUM SCALLYWAG

2 oz. light rum
1 oz. dark rum
2 oz. orange juice
1/2 oz. lemon juice
1/2 oz. almond, or other nut, liqueur
orange slice garnish

Crush enough ice in a blender to make 1/2 cup. Add rum, juice and liqueur. Blend on low speed for 10-15 seconds. Pour into a tall (tom collins) glass, add garnish and it's down the hatch ya' scurvy-bitten bilge rat! Aaaaarrrrgggghhhh!!!!

5) SCURVY CHASER

3 oz. light, golden or dark rum
1 oz. lime juice
2 tbsp. sugar, or simple syrup
mint leaves
club soda
lime wedges

Muddle (mash) 8-10 mint leaves, 2 lime wedges and sugar in a tall (tom collins) glass to release their flavor. Fill the glass with ice, pour in your favorite rum and top with club soda. If it's too tart feel free to add more sugar. Garnish with a lime wedge. It's sure to ward off the scurvy, or get you to a place where you just don't care, matey.

6) PATENTED PIRATE PANTS REMOVER

3 oz. overproof rum
2 oz. coffee liqueur
1 oz. heavy cream (optional)

Pour ingredients into a short (old-fashioned) glass filled with ice and prepare
to lose your pantaloons, me hearties!
They're much too confining anyway.

7) RUM AHOY!

1 oz. light rum
1 oz. golden rum
1 oz. dark rum
1 oz. coconut rum
1/2 oz. lemon juice
club soda
lemon slice & maraschino cherry garnish

Mix rum and lemon juice over ice in a
shaker. Strain into a tall (tom collins)
glass 1/2 filled with ice, top off with
soda and garnish with lemon slice
and cherry. Then make ready to sail,
heave ho, all sheets to the wind and
last one up the rigging gets a cutlass
up his rudder! NOTE: this is authentic
pirate gibberish. Honest.

8) SEA DOG

3 oz. golden rum
1/2 oz. sloe gin
1/2 oz. sweet vermouth
1/2 oz. lemon juice
1/2 oz. passion fruit syrup
dash of Angostura bitters
orange peel & maraschino cherry
garnish

Mix rum, sloe gin, vermouth, juice,
syrup and bitters over ice in a shaker.
Strain into a short (old-fashioned)
glass, twist juice from orange peel into
the drink then drop it in and add the
cherry garnish. Then enjoy, ya'
old salty dog.

9) KEELHAULER

2 oz. dark rum
1 oz. overproof rum
1/2 oz. maraschino cherry liqueur
2 oz. grapefruit juice
2 oz. pineapple juice

Mix all ingredients over ice in a shaker.
Strain into a tall (tom collins) glass 1/2
filled with ice and blow the man down.
This one's sure to scrape the barna-
cles off your bottom, me hearties!

10) BUCCANEER

3 oz. dark rum
1 oz. spiced rum
dash of Angostura bitters
maraschino cherry garnish

Pour rum and bitters into a short (old-fashioned) glass filled with ice and drop in the cherry. This cocktail's a shot across the bow that'll shiver yer timbers and send you right up the rigging, swabby!

APPENDIX: KNOW YOUR RUMS
(YA' RUMMIES)

Rum is a versatile spirit produced in many styles, in many places. The principle producers are Puerto Rico, which provides the majority consumed in the U.S., the Virgin Islands, Dominican Republic, Haiti, Cuba, Barbados, Guyana, Martinique, Jamaica, Trinidad, Java, India, the Philippines and, of course, the U.S.A. and Canada.

What follows is a brief overview of the various kinds of rum. Please note this is by no means all there is to know on the topic. In fact the Booze Fairy encourages you to do your homework and rigorously explore the vast "rum-scape" for yourself.

TYPES & STYLES

LIGHT RUM – also called White or Clear rum, is essentially the colorless distillate with minimal aging in non-charred oak or stainless steel casks. It has a milder flavor and lighter body than darker rums. Mostly used to make cocktails that don't need a strong rum flavor, just a nice kick, often as a substitute for vodka.

GOLDEN RUM – ages in charred oak barrels, previously used to age whiskey. Over time the rum mellows, taking on an amber color and a more flavorful profile than light rum. Enjoyed neat, on the rocks, or in cocktails where a stronger rum flavor is desired. Golden rum is often aged several years or more and some coloring may be added to provide consistency. Flavors vary with the length of aging and type of oak barrel used.

DARK RUM - is a catch-all term given to a range of rums, from golden to black, as well as to rums that are aged in charred oak barrels for extended periods. Again, the length of aging and type of barrel affects the smoothness and flavor.

BLACK RUM - is the darkest, most full-bodied rum lending bold tropical flavors to cocktails and cooking. Black rum is often used to balance the flavors of drinks against the dryer notes from white, golden and spiced rums. Most black rums are made from molasses and retain much of its rich flavor. They're sometimes colored with burnt caramel to achieve consistently dark hues and enhanced flavor.

SPICED RUM - as the name suggests is rum flavored with spices. Much like infused vodkas, the high alcohol content of rum allows it to take on the tropical flavors of spices and herbs which it can then impart to cocktails, or simply add to its flavor when enjoyed straight. Spiced rums offer a wide variety of spice flavors and styles, both full proof and lower proof liqueurs.

FLAVORED RUM - like spiced rums, these are rums infused with vanilla or fruit flavors such as coconut, mango, watermelon and orange. Basically, they save you the step of adding the actual ingredient into fruity rum cocktails, or they can be consumed straight as a liqueur. Like spiced rums, flavored rums offer a wide range of styles, both full proof and lower proof liqueurs.

OVERPROOF RUM – are rums that contain higher concentrations of alcohol than the typical 80 to 100 proof rums and are often labeled as overproof. Modern distillation produces a spirit that is as high as 190 proof. After aging and blending, most rums are diluted with water to reach the standard 80 to 100 proof level. Overproof rums can be used to create flaming cocktails, or just add an extra booze punch. Due to their powerful dehydrating effect, drinking them straight is not recommended even by the Booze Fairy.

PREMIUM AGED RUM – is aged for a long time to achieve a superior flavor and smoothness. They're often the distillery's finest mature rums, blended to achieve a complex and distinctive flavor. A good example of this style are Puerto Rican añejo rums which are aged six years or more. Of course, all this time and care means they are best enjoyed neat, on the rocks or with a splash of water to "open" them up. It also means the distiller passes on the extra production cost to you.

VINTAGE RUM – while most rum sold in the U.S. is blended, some unique rums are bottled from specific vintage years of production. Vintage rums most often come from the French islands of the West Indies, where the growing season is short. Boutique producers are bringing more vintage rums to the market every year. These rums tend to be made in limited quantities and are highly prized by serious rum aficionados. Like premium aged rums, they are best enjoyed neat.

NAVY RUM ~ is the traditional dark, full-bodied style rum associated with the British Navy whose daily rum ration dates back to 1655 when the British fleet captured Jamaica. Also called Limeys for their use of limes to prevent scurvy, British sailors discovered rum traveled aboard ship better than French brandy. Said brandy was also often difficult to get because the two countries were usually doing their level best to kill each other.

RHUM AGRICOLE ~ is a specific kind of rum made from sugar cane juice, mostly in the French territories of the Caribbean especially Martinique. It's also produced in Guadeloupe, Marie-Galante and St. Barths, Reunion and its Indian Ocean neighbor Mauritius. Rhums made in Haiti from cane juice may also be called agricole.

CACHAÇA (kah-SHA-sah) ~ is the beloved, no frills rum of Brazil and one of the world's most popular. Made from sugar cane juice, cachaça is often bottled with little or no aging. Its full-flavored profile and potent kick are mostly popularly enjoyed in mixed drinks such as Brazil's national cocktail the caipirinha (kai-pee-REEN-yah).

AQUARDIENTE ~ which translates to "burning water" or "fire water" is a Caribbean and South American spirit made from sugar cane, or cane juice. It can be flavored with various herbs and fruits. Much like American moonshine it's not aged and is often cut with water, 'cuz drinking it straight will really curl your toes. Rumor has it that's why the Booze Fairy needs his curly booties.

144

CLOSING THOUGHTS

The Booze Fairy hopes you enjoy his collection of rum cocktail recipes. Like all things Booze Fairy, there may not be a whole lot of what you'd call coherent thought to it, but what fun would it be if there were? Hopefully it'll come in handy at your next hootenanny or rager, and hopefully you'll have some fun exploring the wide world of rum. In closing the Booze Fairy has just on thing to say, "you're welcome, boys and girls!"

Join the party and get the whole collection of Booze Fairy books!

THE BOOZE FAIRY'S
Drinking Holidays Personal Premium
Customized Super Fun Official Cocktail Recipe
Book: Unlimited Edition

 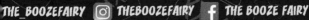